Pieces of Me

Shane Williams

BookLeaf Publishing

Presentation by *BookLeaf Publishing*

Web: www.bookleafpub.com

E-mail: info@bookleafpub.com

ISBN: 9789395026611

First edition 2022

DEDICATION

To the Old Me... Thank You for your resilience, sacrifice, and pain. I hope I make you proud. To the Future Me... I wish you all the happiness, success, and peace your heart desires.

ACKNOWLEDGEMENT

In publishing my first piece of work a lot of people come to mind that without them, this would all be impossible. I would first like to thank my parents Darnell Williams and Sharnetta Williams for creating such a creative woman. To the Mom I didn't know I needed Mary Williams thank you for loving me, accepting me, encouraging me, and praying over my life. You have helped see me through some very dark hours as well as celebrate alongside me for some of my greatest moments. Your wisdom and patience are things I admire most about you and I hope to have more of as I grow. To my Poppa Bear Eric Burwell I can not say thank you enough. Every time I call you are always there for me no matter what it is. Your love and kindness towards me from the very first moment we met has always warmed my heart, and set the standard of how I wanted any man that claimed to love me to treat my children. You take time out of your busy life to just teach me, encourage me, and making sure I'm not being deceived by the tricks of the enemy. And lastly but certainly never least My Aunt NeeNay Renee Lathern Kinjo although you are actually my cousin you have been a mother, a friend, a teacher, and truly a staple to me. As a child you were always there for me loving me, getting me every weekend, doing my hair and buying all the cutest outfits. Growing up still there right by my side teaching me, guiding me, showing me all the ladylike things your Amazing Mother Sheila Lathern taught you. Then when you noticed me heading down the wrong road in high school you took me in to show me a better way. You will never know how much that meant to me and I will forever be grateful for that decision.

To my amazing sisters Sharese Williams and Lauren Rowlette I love you more than a million words could ever express. Rese you are my Wombmate, A1 day one, Ridah, and best friend. You have been there for me in so many ways, and even though I wanted to be an only child forever I'm really glad I have you. L you've been such an inspiration in my life I don't even know where to begin, I remember crying and memorizing all the lyrics of your song 'She Speaks' when I had my first heartbreak. Your creativity is out of this world and I admire you so much. Even though I definitely never wanted a step sister, being the biggest Symantyx fan ever I was honored to call you family and the love you've shown me has made us blood. It can't get no thicker, Love You A Millon Pink Starburst! To My loving husband who is my biggest supporter and #1 Fan, Jason Woods life would be so much harder without you in it. I want to thank you for the life you work so hard to provide for our family. For the way you've come into my life and shown me the kind of love I've waited so long for I could never repay, but I acknowledge your sacrifice and dedication to becoming a better man for me. You have elevated my confidence in myself and changed this Spoiled Princess to a even more Spoiled Queen. I acknowledge and appreciate the Patience, Pain, Pleasure, and Progress you've deposited in my life. IFLY until the day I die.

There are 3 influential women in my life that I must acknowledge next for my education in being A Lady, and A Mother. Alicia Blackledge, Reba Hunter, and Gladys Leathers you all have shown me so much from the way you live your lives. Alicia you are my favorite cousin period not just on my dad's side. You taught me how to cook and clean and keep a house up as the woman should. You carried me everywhere you went and always made sure I had whatever I needed. Still to this day you are in my life to vent to and teach me and I value all you are and do. Reba you were a crucial part of raising me when my mother wasn't in the house. You helped with homework, kept my sense of responsibility in tact, and taught me that even without a man any children I Bear was my priorities. Gladys aka Aunt Mussy you were the first person I went to when I found out I was carrying a son. You were my image of what a strong woman looks like. The way you demand respect and the love your son has for you above all else is what I wanted for mine as well. Thank you for all the advice, love, and most importantly examples of how a God fearing mother carries herself.

In closing I'd like to also thank a few friends who have been with me for a very long time. Been shoulders to cry on, ears to vent to, and arms to embrace me. Nicole Sellars(formerly Havis), Jessica Davis and Samuel Clemons your are true friends to the end and I couldn't imagine every losing you.

Thank you to all my friends, family, and fans who believed in me and gave me kind words through this process. I appreciate you so much.

PREFACE

I can recall 21 monumental moments in my lifetime that really shaped and molded me into the person I've become today. Some of these memories were amazing to remember like the birth of my children, or a healthy relationship. Others not so much, but those were the ones that showed me how much strength i had inside of me. Everything I've been through has taught me valuable lessons about who I want to be. I've learned so much about me in these last 34 years, yet I keep surprising me every day.

The Birth of Mikey

My First Born Son
You came into my world so unexpected
And like the whirlwind you are you instantly
swept me up
Everything I did or said was about you, I
couldn't wait to meet you
My favorite singer died right after I found out
you were a boy
So I just knew I'd have a Lil' Mike to carry
around and love forever
Your entrance in this world almost took me out,
but you got one strong mama
It did however keep me away from you for 3
very long critical bonding months, then made
the next few a physically painful bonding
experience
Still I've never loved someone more
The minute I could hold you I wanted to
The day I came home I had to be taken care of,
yet I still wanted to take care of You
For me having you in my life meant truly loving
someone forever no matter what
People change, they grow, they learn, they want
different things
But a Mother's Love never changes.

It is limitless, and ever growing, extremely
powerful, almost magical at times
You gave me a power my heart needed to repair
itself and love again
Because of your DNA I always knew you'd be a
very bright individual with wide range of
abilities.
Thankfully you balance creativity and ingenuity
beautifully and I'm so proud
Even at such a young age you have already set
out, and accomplished a goal that would take
most people a lifetime to do.
You're an awesome big brother to your little
brother and your little sister
They both want to be just like you when they
grow up
Because you're one amazing kid, My First Born
King

The Birth of Mani

My Miracle Baby
My Second Chance, Do-Over, Reset Button,
Against all odds, and I do mean All.
You had a 7% chance of conception, You were
born almost two months early,
You had to be taken home on a heart machine,
and constantly monitored
And Colic was the cherry on top
You cried day and night, then
You cried night and day
But over time you grew to be the cutest little ball
of fuss I'd ever seen
Then I repaid you all those tears as your
precious face was my only joy through my
darkest hours
Ironically within the first year of your life
combined we probably shed enough tears to fill
a river
But then it all changed and you became the
driving force in my life
You knew your ABC's and 123's ahead of
schedule and continued to grow and amaze me
everyday
In just 5 short years of your life we have seen
each other through so much,

And I can tell how much you love me.
My Love for you is limitless and continues to
grow as you do
It's not always easy being me but you make it so
worth it.
I've never met a child more aware and
empathetic in my life
You give me constant praise and approval for the
smallest things,
And allow me my space but still somehow
shower me with love when I'm down
You are one magical kid and I hope you know it
You hold an awesome power over me Manuel
You've saved my life in more ways than one
So I will make sure yours is always filled with
all the joy and love in the world
There's nothing I wouldn't do for you, My Son
My dream came true.

The Death of Patricia

It hit me like a ton of bricks, took all the wind out of my sails, and I felt like I was drowning all of a sudden. As I was driving down the street literally a few blocks away from the hospital where I just kissed my grandmother good night, I got the worse phone call of my life. She was gone. The woman that raised me was now gone, and in a car full of people I never felt more alone. My husband pulled over into a parking lot and got out of the car to console me. It hurt so bad like a million tiny needles all over, I swore every limb went to sleep all at the same time. I don't know how long we stayed in that parking lot but every second after that call started to blend together. There was an endless flow of family and friends stopping by, offering condolences and cooking food. We partied day and night to celebrate the life of the party no longer being here with us at the Clark Williams Household, but it just wasn't the same. In her room you could find all of the grand kids occupying their favorites spaces, mine was her recliner or the floor of her closet. I closed myself in surrounded by the smell of her and bawled my eyes in the fetal position. I wasn't ready to start

living life without her, and in that moment I
didn't know how I ever could be. How could I
possibly go on without my lifeline? She was
everything to me and then some. I was her first
grand child and a girl when she'd only raised
boys, so naturally she used to tell people I was
her child. I was her secretary when she would
leave work early to be with us , she'd have me
typing up all her notes into a report like I went to
college for social work and knew what I was
doing. I was her calendar, constantly keeping up
with dates and events we had coming up and
places we needed to be. I was her personal
assistant, keeping track of what we needed to
buy for the house and going out with her on pay
day to get it. I will always remember how we
had to eat before shopping for groceries, she
would say "Never go into a grocery store on an
empty stomach, you'll buy the whole damn
store". She was always schooling me, guiding
me, showing me what she wanted out of life for
me. We talked about marriage and raising
children. She wanted me to have fun and make
mistakes so I would also have something to give
to the next generation. She was my live in
Manual on how life was supposed to flow.
Without her here to refer to I knew I'd be lost,
but I never knew that loss felt this way. I had
family members that passed before her even

some I was rather close to, and I cried and felt sadness and mourned their lives. This was nothing like that, compared to every other funeral I've ever attended they might as well have been strangers. On the inside I felt like one of those scenes from a movie where some woman is crying uncontrollably into the casket of her loved one. However as her first grand child and daughter I played my role with poise and grace. An angelic vision in all white down to the shoes. I wore a sleeveless white lace pants jumpsuit with a long white cape and a classic single string of pearls with pearl earrings to match, completing the look with all white pumps and a high braided crown. As I flowed down the isle to kiss My Angel goodbye the tears just flowed, I felt weaker with every step forward and could barely feel my body by the time I reached her. I braced myself on the white satin of the casket and leaned in to kiss her forehead. I whispered " I love you so much, I'm sorry I wasn't there and I know you waited for me. Rest Well My Love. We got it from here." I then turned to the front row to hug her brothers and sisters and my dad and uncle then took my place next to them. Her home church was filled to the rafters with people from all walks of her life paying their respect and saying their final goodbyes. She was truly loved and sorely missed. Nobody could ever take her place or fill a third of her shoes. Patricia Clark was the life of the party, even in death she had one epic send off. A few months before her passing she had a grand " give me my flowers while I'm still here" event where we showered her with love and appreciation on and around her birthday. Her friends and family all showed up and showed out to eat, sing, dance, and honor who P. Clark was in their lives. We didn't know at the time this would be her final hoorah, but I'm sure she did. She was very ill surrounding the weekend of that party and shortly after it passed she was admitted to the hospital and they told us it was Stage III cancer of the Stomach. How long must she have kept this secret from us to be at stage III already and it was only our first time hearing the word Cancer. It completely threw my world for a loop and I found it near impossible to bring myself to her bedside. The woman who had been there for me all my life was slowly dying and I didn't even have a clue she was sick. This isn't one of the proudest moments of my life because I was very selfish and inconsiderate to one of the most selfless human beings that ever walked this earth. That woman touched so many lives and took in so many people it'd take a whole other book to mention it all. She raised two boys into men, took in five grandchildren from them and practically raised them all as siblings under the same roof, and then got to enjoy the life of her first two grandsons born under her roof as well. She had a full life of working hard everyday, raising a wonderful family, and traveling all over the world. For weeks she was up talking and I thought she would just come home and go to Cancer Treatment of America Center and we could turn this around. I didn't want to face reality at the time because she was just in the hospital not too long before that and came home fine so I was sure she would this time as well. I talked to her a few times on the phone and always talked to my siblings when they got in from the hospital. Then my dad called and said it wasn't looking good for her, he wanted the family all together to possibly say goodbye. The pain that hit me that day was unbearable. I felt like a mountain of boulders was dropped on top of my lungs and all the air within was trapped with no hope of escape. My heart ached and mind raced all through the night. The next day I gathered my strength and made my way to my Angel's side. Most of the family was there and there as a lot of praying and waiting. As the night was coming to a close people said their goodbyes and started to leave. I was downstairs visiting someone else before i left but i wanted to say goodnight too so i convinced her nurses to

let me in for a min to say goodnight and turn on
her music for her. I said a quick prayer and
kissed her cheek shortly after she took her last
breath and before i could even make it more than
a mile away from the hospital i got the call. She
waited for me all night held on until we had the
chance to be alone and once I was gone she let
go. It took me too long and I carried the guilt
that she may have suffered even one second
longer than she had to, but I knew even in her
death she was showing me that she'd always be
with me. I loved more than anyone I know and it
was now clear that she held just as much for me
if not more.

The Death of Burnetta

Burnetta Frenchy Hunter had no cut cards and
played no games.
She would give it to you straight and always
spoke straight from the heart.
The little lady with the big attitude that would
finish whatever you start.
She was larger than life and in her mind always
right.
But turned to a little baby during her first flight.
Burnetta Frenchy Hunter had a heart made of
pure gold.
Every December she played Santa to her entire
family,
and we're not exactly 4 or 5 deep truth be told.
Her Easter baskets that started out for her
grandchildren quickly took off as a business
once people saw how beautiful and advanced
they were.
And the friendship outreach family were the first
ones to order from her.
Yeah that was just Netta, everything she put her
mind to she filled with love, beauty, and grace.
But if you ever crossed a Hunter it was her you
had to face.

She always wanted everyone to come together
and eat; she'd provide the laughs.
But as much as she could build you up her
words could also cause a grown man's
bloodbath.
Justly named after her mother she carried that
Burnetta torch with ease.
She didn't tip toe, sugar coat, lolligag, or people
please.
She had many jobs in this family, and she took
them all in stride.
To have known her was to love her and as her
family we're taking that with pride. Simply put
Burnetta Frenchy Hunter was absolutely the
best,
And knowing that we're glad God gave his
Angel A Day of Rest.

I Love Forever Grandma,
May you continue to rest in sweet heavenly
peace, and protect me from up above.

Burnetta 'Frenchy' Hunter Sunrise: April 29,
1951 - Sunset: January 4, 2020

Velcro

From the first moment I met You,
I knew right then I would get you.
You were so Smooth, but so Shy
Beautiful just my type, and you did all the things
I like
But i was also very taken,
And your hand in mine just replaced his.
We did all the things we should not, you always
make me hot, and its starting to blow up the
spot.
But we kept, and we kept on going Hard
Now i cant, Cant let you go... I Want It
Stuck on you don't know what to do, its like
we're pushing and you're pulling
But all I see is You, You, You. Yet I Want You.
And now You got me Always
I want it I need it you know I gotta have it. I
love it I crave it your love is like a habit
i want it I need it you know I gotta have that its
coming cant stop it you know you wanna grab
that
Now as time goes on and bonds grow strong,
You fuck with me, I fuck with you, the long way
and you know it

I ain't scared to show it off, posting selfies on the
gram
I'm the Queen don't touch my crown, I'll go
crazy I'll go ham
but then I calm down I know well be alright
You want something real, that don't happen
overnight
I need to know you gone ride for me, fight for
me, you gone protect my heart, you gonna
always do whats right for me.
So we'll keep, and we'll keep on going hard
cause I can't, can't let you go I Want It
Stuck on you don't know what to do
You fuck with i fuck with the long way and you
know it
But all I see is You, You, You
I'm the queen don't touch my crown I'll go crazy
I go ham
And now you got me Always

Need You

Sitting here crying all night long
I really hate you're gone, need you i cant go on.
And you gave me life you taught me to be strong
I really hate you're gone need you i cant go on.
I wish i knew how to just be, without you right
here with me.
I wish i could see your hopes and dreams for me
come true and just be...
The me you always wanted me to be
You've prepared me and you've shown me things
so i could be a queen.
I'm so grateful that i had someone like you in my
life.
Call that mission completed you did it, you did
it.
And though these tears keep falling I keep
stalling It's selfish I get it I'll admit it but   I
Need You yeah I Need You so badly,
(and though the people who stuck with me love
and support me its true)
They Don't Love Me Like You Do
I Need You yeah I Need You so badly
(and yeah these tears keep falling i keep stalling
my heart is so black and blue)
They Don't Love Me Like You Do

I keep praying one day I'll wake up and It's all
just just a dream
I'll get back My Favorite Lady, My Gma, My
Heart, My Queen
yeah It's been a little while now since you went
away
but my heart still feels it was yesterday
I Need You yeah I Need You so badly,
(and though the people who stuck with me love
and support me its true)
they don't love me like you do
I Need You yeah I Need You so badly
(and yeah these tears keep falling i keep stalling
my heart is so black and blue)
They Don't Love Me Like You Do
Sitting here crying all night long
I really hate you're gone Need You I cant go on

The Tragic Tale of Maddison

I saw you in my dreams as the child I never had. The possibility of a happy and simple life full of love and hope was what we shared. We played in the yard together running around until I couldn't breathe. I named you Maddison Vanea Funn but everyone called you Maddy, and you looked just like me. You had soft golden brown curls, eyes that resembled sunflowers, and big bright pink cheeks. If only in my dreams I would make a perfect home for you, something like the one I grew up in. It was big and blue, had a wrap around porch with a white swing, and in the yard was a simple kiddie pool, a tire swing, and a tree house. I had a lovely garden full of fruits and vegetables that we spent hours in. Your father spent many hours at work providing for us but when he was around you lit up like a Christmas tree, and in his eyes you could do no wrong. He looked at you as his Savior and you looked at him as your Superman. Being the perfect balance of both your mother and father was the biggest blessing in itself because it showed how evenly yoked they were. To be born of pure love and raised with two stable present parents was a very rare thing in my generation so I never really had an example to look to. But for you that wasn't a pain you'd ever know. You always felt love. You always had everything you needed, and most of the things you wanted too. You were truly a happy carefree child. I never saw you shed a tear, or fall and get a bruise. I never saw you being scolded for doing something wrong. I never saw fear, anger, worry, or doubt on your precious face. In my dreams your life was perfect, or maybe it wasn't but it was what I imagined my life would look like if it were perfect. If I had a chance to hold you in my arms. If I made a different choice. I dreamed of all the perfect decisions in my life I never made blended together. My first born beautiful baby girl, my fulfilling career as a writer, my wholesome marriage to a decent God fearing man, and a big house on Easy Street. But this isn't a fairy-tale my love, I'm saddened that your story as most of mine are is a tragedy. I never got to know you or love you because all I could see was the harsh world you would have been born into. I loved your father dearly and I do believe he would have loved you all the same, But he wasn't mine to claim. We had a beautiful story filled with love and kindness, and a passion unmatched by any other. I was a few years younger than he was and when we met in school and there was no possibility of being

anything other than friends. We connected on a
spiritual level instead, he would wait for my
train with me and have bible study right in the
metro station. Any time I had a problem I talked
to him about it because I knew he would give a
faith based solution. He was my voice of reason
and my school yard crush. Years later he saved
my life. As I was going through the worse
relationship I had ever been in he stepped into
my life once again and brought me right back to
the old days when I used to go to church 4 times
a week like clockwork. He changed my life, he
prayed for me, he cried for me, and he wiped my
tears away. Then one night he got really close to
seeing all of me, and i tried to push him away.
HE was digging up things that i have trusted
anyone with and wasn't prepared to do so then. I
later found out that this was also the night he
became unsure of me as the woman he was
meant to be with, because he knew i was hiding
things and felt pushed away. That one fateful
night changed so many lives. I was broken and
too ashamed to say why, but as he consoled me
we conceived you, then continued with a public
relationship in front of my family. We went to
church together, always sat next to each other,
and then ate with family and friends afterwords.
He would spend the night at my grandmother's
house often just to hold me through the night.

We washed each others hair, and got each other
ready for work in the mornings. We taught each
other how to cook our favorite dishes. His
buttermilk fried chicken is to die for. Things
moved so quickly and before you knew it I was
seeing his Facebook post announcing his
marriage to another woman. I felt sick to my
stomach then found out you and him were both
the reason why. You weren't supposed to be born
out of wed lock and if I was completely honest
with him the night you were conceived he would
have never have married another woman,
inadvertently abandoning his true wife and child.
Once again i was in a place where i just couldn't
be honest about what was going on in my own
life. What would people say? What would my
own church think of me? 80% of the members
were blood related, surely this would tarnish the
family. I wept uncontrollably, I didn't know what
else to do. Your father had ruined my life no
matter what decision I made. If I chose to have
you I would be forever subjecting you to a
church scandal, hearing people make up lies and
rumors because they didn't know the truth,
forced to lie to you to protect the image of your
father in your eyes, because he would have
definitely been in your life no matter what. If I
chose to abort the only person I thought I would
be hurting was me. I was wrong. You not being

here has caused just as much if not more pain
that we would have endured if I gave you life. I
didn't see that taking his decision away would
have hurt him. I didn't see him pulling away and
feeling unsure of our relationship. I didn't see
having you in spite of all the reasons not to was
all the love you'd ever need in this world. I didn't
see the beauty and potential in your eyes, and
the many gifts and talents you could have shared
with the world. Maddison I am so very sorry that
I put everyone's needs before my own, and if I
could turn back the hands of time I would chose
You. If only I could fix the cracks in the
foundation of your creation i could have saved
your father from a loveless marriage to the
wrong woman and years of bad judgement and
heartbreaks for your mother.

Easter Sunday/ Monday @ The Zoo

Pastels, and fresh hair do's
White Church gloves for Sunday Morning
Service
Pictures with the all the family in front of 2nd
New St. Paul
Then a bomb Dinner back at home
Preparations for the next day at the zoo always
came in the late night hours
We'd stay up all night boiling eggs, making
sandwiches, and decorating baskets
There was always extra cousins around to play
with and she never left them out
She would have us decorate old shoe boxes, then
stick some string grass in it and fill it with all the
things our baskets had in them
Monday morning we set off to The Zoo for some
Easter Family Fun
The Smithsonian National Zoological Park in
Washington DC to be exact
We had picnics, live music, games, rolling down
grass hills, and so many animals
But most important we had family
This tradition started way before my time when
my grandmother was a little girl

Her parents and all their siblings would meet at
the zoo the day after Easter Sunday for a free
and fun way to bond and stay connected as a
family.
My grandmother valued traditions so much and
was The Best Matriarch a family could ever ask
for.
I aspire to be more like her when I'm older and
have generations behind me
I want them to tell stories of how we do it this
way because it was passed down from my
childhood and teach their children
I don't know if it will be Easter Sunday at the
church house
Easter Monday at the Zoo
One Big Family Summer Trip a year
Thanksgiving Roulette between Hosts each year
Superbowl Parties or
Fireworks after a cookout on the 4th of July
But I will pass on something that brought me as
much joy as seeing all her family together at the
zoo brought My Grandmother.

High School Sweethearts

The first man I ever thought I'd marry wasn't a man at all when we met. I met Joel Davis in the hallways of middle school heading to lunch. He was tall, athletic, and the best shade of brown you'd ever seen. He stood out from every other boy that wanted to talk to me. So naturally I wanted to talk to him. I ran straight into him and when he pulled me back in to keep me from falling I raised my head to look up at him and smiled. "Thank You" I said. He replied in the smoothest voice ever "Anytime Shorty, be careful". Within the week we were an item, old school "Do you like me? Do you want to be my girlfriend? Check Yes or No" note right in class. I was hooked, from that day I was at every game no questions asked and he attended every recital, play, or show I was in without fail. We shared a locker, we arrived at school together, we left school together. By the time prom rolled around we had been dating for a solid year and a half, so it was just assumed that we'd go together but he didn't see the need to ask me because we were already together. It was the first time he ever really hurt me, we never really argued or saw things differently before. We just fit together, without the drama that school relationships usually include. This was both of our first relationships so all we knew was what we've seen from our families and television. I wasn't a guy so Bro Code was a foreign language to me, but somehow I had stepped right in the middle of whole war on the Bro Code ethics. One of Joel's teammates decided to ask me to Prom since he hadn't and I made the mistake of mentioning how I was looking forward to a grand gesture. The next day he gave me that grand gesture on the stage of the cafeteria with everyone watching. As soon as I seen Joel's face I knew this would be bad for us but I never thought it was as serious as he did. We both hurt each other and were acting like complete kids about it. We hadn't yet grasped the concept of communication in relationship and letting the other person in on how you were feeling. So instead of fixing things I went to our prom with William Epps and he went with Rachael Robbins. William was the perfect gentleman and tried to make the best of a very awkward situation but it divided our whole group of friends. Originally we all would've been going in on a joint limo but William had his uncle drive us in his all black Cadillac and we stepped out looking like Royalty. I wore a gorgeous burgundy ball gown with gold accessories and curly pin up. He wore a deep Purple tux with black suede shoes and gold watch. When we arrived I saw multiple friends taking pictures together on the steps and the music was on point. The night was all smooth sailing until talks of an after party was being circulated among the different cliques. I didn't want for Will and Joel to end up in an altercation so i decided that we would just go out to eat and back to my best friends house for the night. We hit the IHOP in Hyattsville MD and ordered the world. They were smoking in the car ride over so by the time we got seated i was starving. Sean one of Joel's friends who was like a brother to me called and asked if i knew about the party in the city and that i needed to get there right away. So i asked if anybody wanted to crash the after party with me and we headed over after we were full and satisfied. When i walked in the party i didn't see Joel anywhere and that was hard for him to hide in a crowd, so i started asking around. I ran into my neighbor and close friend Jess Davis and asked her what she was doing on this side. She said she came through to check on her cousin and ended up getting in a fight with this hoodrat chick in his face. I had no idea she was related to my boyfriend until she said his nickname. She told me he was locked in a room with the girl now, and I lost it. With Jess on my heels I stormed through the house, opening every door, searching for my man and that skank. When I finally found them she was sitting on a bed in front of him crying. I called her out of her name and with a running start tried to lunge at her but Joel caught me mid air and left the room. He stomped down the hallway with me kicking and screaming the whole time, then placed me in the bathroom to calm down and talk. "What the fuck was that?" I shouted. He retorted "What you jumping to conclusions and literally jumping on a girl that just got assaulted? I was wondering the same thing. What the fuck was you thinking Boo, like come on do you really think I would cheat on you over a stupid fucking prom!" His words were interrupted by the sounds of commotion and we rushed to check it out. There was my girl back at it with Rachael thinking the same thing I was a minute ago. She was pounding that poor girl to a pulp, but in Jess' defense Rachael's mouth was known to be a real problem. She just had one of those personalities that screamed fight me, even if that isn't what she meant at all. I honestly felt like that was the only reason he went with her anyway, because lets face it Joel Davis could have any girl he wanted. He had the gorgeous, sweet, smart, and talented girl in the bag. So what else could he possibly want? That's right

the loud mouth street smart chick. I guess its
only natural to want you don't already have.
Looking back now that may have been the
reason we always seemed to drift apart. I dated
Joel throughout almost every stage of my life
and each time it was picture perfect. We just fit
together appearance and personality wise, we
compliment and accentuate each other in ways
that no one else did. In high school our bond
really solidified. We were a little older and much
wiser now. We weren't ready for conflicting
complex emotions in middle school, and our
communication was abysmal. So the first thing
we did was build an open honest line of
communication, and we kept that line busy. We
talked day and night when we weren't in school,
it drove our parents crazy, but we didn't care. We
just wanted to be closer to each other, to know
how the other was feeling or dealing with life.
Our dates at this stage in life was lunch time or
practices after school, and occasionally a family
event. We would play Uno and Spades with our
friends and I loved watching him on the court in
and out of school. I dreamed that we would
finish high school together and I would push
him into the NBA tryouts every year. I used to
fantasize about being a basketball wife way
before the show was created. I saw me fly as
ever court-side cheering my man on, taking

flights all the time to see his away games, and eventually making a little starter team of our own. I dreamed of a Forever with him and to be honest I've had a lot of dreams since high school but Forever with a man wasn't on the list anymore. Every single man that has walked into my life after my high school sweetheart I could imagine walking right back out. I cant honestly say it jaded me either because time after time we ended things and picked them right back up years later like nothing had happened. We never carried our scars from other people into our union, we would talk about them and fill the other in on the things that's happened since we last spoke. The toxic pattern of couples being on again off again wasn't what we shared, it was more like a familiar comfortability that reignited whenever we talked and neither of us wanted to lose it. Two years after my first born son arrived we walked into each others lives again and this was the first time we acknowledged that we just couldn't leave each other alone for good. Once again i saw forever in his eyes and it felt good. I knew that no matter how much life would hurt me, or break me down there would always be one person who not only still saw the good in me, but was able to bring a little bit of that old me to the surface. My High School Sweetheart will always hold a special key to my heart. Who knows if the story is ever over when you always want to see the main characters win. Sometimes winning looks like different people for them and sometimes the victory is finding their way back home again.

The Man That Made My Heart

The first day I met Vincent Chopard was unlike any day I've ever lived before or since. It was something straight out of a cheesy Hollywood movie, stunts included. I can remember how I felt, what I was going through, and how it seemed like the universe just stepped in and gave me a boost I didn't know I needed. I just recently moved away from my beloved city to the suburbs of MD, but I was still making a daily commute to DC for school with all my friends. This was different for me, I couldn't hang out and lose track of time because you had to time MD buses just right. In DC you always knew another one would be along shortly and you'd probably even talk right through that one passing too. But my new buses only ran every hour or longer sometimes and stopped running way earlier than I was used to. I felt like an outcast allowed to see my friends for a few short hours and then leave everything and everyone behind like they didn't matter. Only I was the one who no longer mattered, I was the one who couldn't keep up with talk in school because I missed everything they were even talking about. I needed something new and amazing, my heart longed for an adventure so talk worthy I would be the News in school. I went out for a walk to clear all my racing thoughts about how I would elevate my life. Surrounded by big beautiful homes some totaling close to a million dollars I had the nerve to think I needed the boost in my life. I was gorgeous, young, and extremely calculated, everything in my life made a statement about the woman I would become. It was intentional to be the best version of myself I could be. I kind of wish I still had that mentality and drive about myself to today, but I do remember that version of me often being associated with the harsh words like Vain, Selfish, Self-Centered, Conceited, Self-Serving, and Materialistic. Some point in my life those were all words I specifically tried to kill about me so going back would just diminish the collective work of the woman I've become today. Without the help of the man in this story I would be nowhere close to the woman I am today. He was the first man I dated and I do mean Man. For legal reasons, as well as my privacy I have changed all the names and some of the events in this story making it a very creative fictional piece. As I walked down the streets of my beautiful gated community I could feel the roar of an engine growing closer and closer to me. It snatched me out of my thoughts and all I could do was imagine my hair blowing in the wind next to the driver. I didn't dare turn around to catch a glimpse but as he passed me I smiled then winked. I didn't who I was more in love with that amazing piece of machinery or the picture of perfection driving it. As soon as our eyes locked he did a crazy complete 360 right there in the middle of the road to come back and talk to me. I was beyond flattered and couldn't get my cheeks to stop glowing no matter what I did. He pulled up in a navy blue Ferrari F430 and slowed his pace this time rolling down the window to talk to me as I walked. "Do you believe in Love at sight or do I have to try that spin again?' He asked confidently. Now in full blown blush mode I stopped to face his car and ask "What can I do for you sir?". He quickly responded "Any chance you have an extra heart? Mine's just been stolen". He was the smoothest talker ever and here I was caught up in the web. It should be noted that although I was barely 17 I had the poise and sophistication of a woman of 21. He gave me his number and suggested I come to soiree he was hosting tonight. It was a school night, but it was also bible study night and i knew my mom would be away for hours tonight. I didn't agree outright but told him I would think about it and let him know. When i got back home my mother was pulling into the driveway and I immediately jumped into character making a way to not end up in church tonight. I was weak and fatigued and i thought some fresh air would help but now I was just outright not feeling well at all and needed some rest if i was gonna make it to school the next day. It worked like a charm, before she left she stopped in my room to check on me and I was nicely tucked away fake sleeping. Once i heard the car leave i sprung into action looking for something to wear to a party that didn't scream underage to his friends. I had somehow fooled him without even trying the question of age never came up, however if I was going to make this man a permanent fixture in my life I had to not only come up with part but perfect and play that part to a T. I could tell right away that Vincent was that new thing I so desperately needed to be on top again. He was a tall, well built, obviously wealthy, and charming man with a soft spot for me and i knew just what to do with soft spots. I chose a simple and elegant pencil skirt paired with a crop top that gave the illusion of a strapless cocktail dress then ran in my mom's room to borrow a great pair of heels and some jewelry. I then called up Mr. Chopard and asked him if he had a date this evening. We joked around for a few minutes and I agreed to accompany him to his party and he'd meet me where we met earlier that day in about a half hour. I took the side exit and left the door unlocked in case i had to sneak in pass my mother tonight it was the only entrance that could get me to my door without her seeing me. Vincent picked me up at the corner and we went on a little joyride getting to know each other before we headed to his place. I found out that he was a mechanic with a passion for fast foreign cars. He would buy them, then soup them up making ultimate racing machines, and cash in heavy with the after hours drag racing community. His life was exciting, thrilling, and just what I needed to rebuild mine. I told him I was a singer, model, and aspiring actress taking some improv classes. He was a very forward and open man that knew what he liked and what he wanted and wasn't afraid to speak his mind freely. When we arrived at his home and pulled into the carport I was amazed I didn't know how many of these vehicles he owned personally but the entire Cul-de-sac was filled with flashy cars and bikes that I imagined belonged to some of the richest snobs in my new neighborhood. He opened my door and reached for my hand. Before we even got to the door I knew just how much he wanted to say screw everyone and get me out of my dress, because he verbally stated as such multiple times plus could not keep his hands off of me. For some reason I knew I was playing with fire but I liked the warmth it provided and the beautiful view of its flames. I didn't see anything wrong with being here and being courted heavily by this handsome man. I didn't see that at the time I was arm candy and some fun for the night. I was still in high school and from my experience this level of attention meant wanting a relationship with a girl, so I turned my Charm and Whit all the way up. I was so overdressed because all of his friends were so down to earth, chill, nerdy, and all grease monkeys at heart. So just being genuinely interested and asking a million questions they wanted to talk about anyways somehow worked for me. I told you the universe aligned this day so nothing could go wrong and I do mean nothing. It was the best party ever and it wasn't even really a party at all just a bunch of his friends over on a Wednesday night. The smoke in the air was thick as hell and I was in paradise off contact alone. The music was so diverse but deep, and being an alleged musician at the time I had to have a diverse appreciation of all art forms. I played my hand effortless all night and succeeded in driving him crazy, I whispered in his ear while grabbing his hand and placing it on my perfect thin waist "Can you handle all these

curves with ease or should I drive?" Barbarian
style he threw me over his shoulder and bid his
friends adieu. He marched all the way up the
stairs and through the house with me up there
and didn't drop me until we reached the master
bed. I felt like he dropped me on top of a
freaking cloud bit could've been the weed too.
He laid down beside me brushed the scar on my
left cheek then lifted my chin until our eyes met
and said the sexiest thing anyone has ever said to
me, "So, tell me your story". I bit my lip and
closed my eyes feeling an instant wave of
euphoria and said "I'm still writing it." The
passion between us gave way and we hungrily
tore each others clothes off, kissing each newly
exposed body part along the way. The way he
looked at me was unlike anything I'd ever seen
before and I wanted this feeling to last forever. I
fell asleep in his arms after a few earth
shattering hours of pure bliss. I thought I was
dreaming and that none of this could have
actually happened to me the same day I declared
it to be so, but that dream jolted me awake like
knife as I saw the hues of deep night starting to
change. I couldn't believe I stayed out all night
surely my mom knew by now I was not still fast
asleep and there is no amount of covering my
little sister could after the jig was up. I quickly
scrambled to get dressed but my clothes were all

disheveled on the account that we took no proper care removing them. I quickly wrote him the sweetest love letter then rushed off home. When I walked in my mother was furious and I knew I had to lie and Lie Fast. I told her was out with some neighborhood kids and we went to a friends house to play video games and I just passed out. She wanted me to point out this friend's house and drove all over the neighborhood looking for it. We never found it of course because I didn't remember what it looked like in the daytime. After I survived that first night and what felt like a lifetime of punishment I knew I had to be more careful if I was going to keep seeing Mr. Chopard, and I fully intended to. I would skip school to be with him during the day. I would stay with friends or even family members I knew wouldn't be up my butt to spend nights with him. I would call and he'd come running Everytime, and with his skills there's no trip he couldn't cut in at least half. No matter where I was or what I needed he came through for me. He even came to fix my mother's flat tire on the side of the road once, it was the weirdest experience ever. I just kept thinking about what would happen if she found out who he really was to me or if he found out how old I was. After a while my parents both knew of Vincent and how madly in love we

were. Vincent also knew I was underage most of
our relationship, he just asked one day out of the
blue. I was honest and he was shocked, but
ultimately impressed. We had a good thing going
and neither of us could keep our hands off each
other. He joined the military and moved a few
times, and we christened every city. I enjoyed
flying out and spending holidays together. I
always imagined that our vacations was what
our life would be like if I were older. On my
18th birthday he went all out, showering me
with expensive gifts and a secret getaway. I
thought this would be the beginning of forever,
but we were closer to the end. He took care of
me for so long, but we had become more of
friends who just happened to enjoy exploring
each other's bodies. There was never any real
heartbreak or tragedy in our relationship and he
was the most honest Man I have ever met. He
taught me so much about living a great carefree
life. Vincent Chopard will always be known as
the man who made my heart because he showed
me the best version of who I wanted to be. When
I was with him I always felt like I was on the set
of a movie because the chemistry was insane
and it was always action packed. He made me
believe a Rom-Com type of love actually existed
in real life and that's the best gift anyone has
ever given me.

A Brother's Love

Your love for me knows no bounds
When I need you you're there
No questions asked
I can depend on your words to ring true no
matter what
You don't sugar coat anything I always get the
real
Any man that comes into my life does so
knowing who stands behind me ain't to played
with.
You Protect me, Direct me, and Respect me
As a man you have set a standard of what I
respect, and expect.
My father schooled us both so you'd think all
My Brother was taught I'd know too
But I still run to you whenever I need A Man's
view on anything
Its because My Brother is my Keeper
He keeps me on my toes
He keeps me Sharp
He keeps me in the know about life and it works
He keeps me in his prayers
He keeps me from going to jail
But the main thing my brother keeps is my faith
that real men

Are Not Extinct!

                    To My Brother E.
Gaines I Love You with Everything In Me

Sister Soulmates

When you hear Soulmate you imagine your husband or wife. Best said by MoonSoulChild "A Soulmate isn't everyone you love throughout your life. A Soulmate is someone who walks into your life and teaches you a love you never felt. It's a connection your heart can't deny. A force that's unbreakable. Not just a lover, A Soulmate comes in all forms, cherish them all." A Soulmate is so much more than just a mate, its the person who sees you for you and who loves you through and through. It is the person you know will always be a part of your life no matter where that life leads you. I was only 5 years when I met my first Soulmate, and I wanted nothing to do with her. She was in the way taking away valuable alone time and she followed me everywhere. As she grew she kind of became like a little best friend and i didn't mind having her around as much. I had someone to tell all my good gossip to, someone to cuddle with after scary movies drove me out my bed, someone who I could tell adored me. I was still cruel, as I said earlier I really wanted that alone time. But every little thing I did I had to think about my Baby Sister. She was my first real obligation and responsibility and it felt very much unwarranted. There was no way I was mature, or even selfless enough to be responsible for a whole extra life. My parents were way too trusting but in that sense they helped our relationship grow. Even though I'm sweet as pie, friendly isn't really a word I would ever use to describe me, but being around each other day in and day out we developed a true friendship. Like true Soulmates do we hold the deepest secrets that we would never tell another soul or very few if we did. We also share a lot of core memories because we lived them together. My first fight was in the hallways of the only school we attended together, and she happened to be walking pass with her class. She jumped out of line to run over and attack the girl which made me fight even harder, cause no way in hell was anybody about to ever touch my baby sister. That wasn't the last fight in our lifetime she's jumped in, and eventually I just let her have it. It's unfair to subject anyone to both of at the same time, because not only are we thinking about hurting you were also protecting our loved one from harm. Aside from the violence we also shared much time creatively together. From music, art, acting, modeling, and even writing we've done it all together, and in most forms i prefer our collaborations to the individual works.

She's always there for me when I need her and that's usually a big sister trait, but being so close we both also have big and little sister qualities. We take turns effortlessly shape shifting into whatever roles the situation requires. We both have two children that just as our cousins were are raised as siblings. The similarities though quite a few isn't what actually makes us soulmates. The irony of the title is that my little sister who stormed this world by surprise, despite my hiding all the catalogs (where I was told babies came from) is the one person who truly knows every version of me and who I've been and loves me the most. This everlasting bond we share whether we like each other that day or not is one of the greatest examples of Sister Soulmates.

To My Only Wombmate
Rese, Love you to the moon and back!

Born From Greatness In His Image/ My First Love

Darnell Lawrence Williams was born and raised in Washington DC with many talents. Some referred to him as a green eyed monster, DC, Malachi, or simply Da Messenger but to me he's just Dad. His courtship with my mom came from a mutual acting company they were both involved with named Everyday Theater. Together they made two beautiful daughters before divorcing. This is the story of Me; his first born, and the love he's given that has shaped my life. From the moment we met he knew he had someone who would always love him and look to him to guide, love, and protect her. He wore that hat with honor knowing I would need every lesson to battle this crazy world. He spoiled me like crazy because he never wanted me to be impressed with a man's wallet and what he could do for me. Taking me out to eat or buying me gifts would never be enough because I was raised by a man who already did those things consistently. He gave me game and taught me how men think so I would always be able to spot a fake from a genuine heart. I was practically his twin growing up, people loved to tell me how much I looked like my daddy, and that was a compliment to say the least. My Dad is one Confident, Stylish, Good Looking, and Charming Man, so if I could also be known for those qualities the world could all be mine. No matter what I've faced he was right there beside me, and still is to this day. There is absolutely nothing that I couldn't tell my father. We have this saying that he's always on my side right, wrong, or indifferent. As long as I'm truly happy and not doing anything unhealthy I always have his support. My father is far from perfect he's had his moments of falling short of the man God called him to be, but just as his for me, my love has never wavered. I see so much of him inside of me its crazy. I was blessed with his good looks, his gift of gab, and most of his talents too. There was a time I hated being so talented because he pushed so hard for greatness. I used to call him the non abusive Joe Jackson, because he was breeding Superstars and making sure we had the work ethic to match. Having my father as my manager was great at times, he wrote all of our material, got us booked for shows, and taught us the behind the scenes work an artist does is more important than hitting the stage. I always carried that perfectionism with me, and believed that if I put in the work my time would come. The talent was natural, the drive was taught, and the inspiration was always him. He's always the first to see anything I write or record. Whenever an opportunity arises he's the first person I share it with to get his opinion. I value my father's words more than any human being in this world. I am his First Love and it shows, nothing moves unless Dad says it does. Growing up there were so many good times I cant even begin to count, but there were also great moments of sadness, and tough lessons learned. I thought in a great father daughter love story I would divide this into 2 stages of my life and share a few of the all time favorites in each stage.

Childhood: Daddy's Little Angel

I was always a daddy's girl to my knowledge. He took me everywhere with him and we had this fun game at the mall that he would make me tell all the prettiest girls that they were so ugly. He treated all the ugliest girls like queens and i treated all the pretty ones like dirt, and before you know it they was all buying out out the mall for the young princess and her daddy. I did whatever he said of course and like a true Mastermind in training we had the whole operation on lock.

We lived on the east coast which meant a January birthday often came with snow. On my 6th birthday we lived down the street from a Pizza Hut back when they use to have a buffet, but the snow was so thick no one wanted to drive or go anywhere. That didn't stop my Daddy from giving his little princess the best birthday ever though. He loaded me up in my little sister's stroller and dashing through the snow we went. Yes we were aware I was far too big for a stroller but that was our only means of transportation. He was teaching me early on that kind of no matter what effort was synonymous with Love. On the way home i broke the stroller and my mom was furious, but to this day its still one of our top fave spoiled moments.
The holidays was always a blast to celebrate with my dad, he always went all out. With very little money he made our childhoods feel like we were beyond privileged kids, and in most ways we were. We got a Hood Snowman with a leather jacket, a Kangol hat, and a cigarette instead of a scarf, top hat, and pipe. We got scary haunted mansions, which was just our house decorated to the nines every Halloween. We had Easter egg hunts and massive water fight wars, that would last for weeks until someone (usually Me) called a truce.

The last greatest treasure of my childhood was a simple game called Trust. You've all played it... you cross your arms, close your eyes, and fall back into the arms of your partner, right? Wrong, the way we played it, you have never played Trust. My dad invented a new way to show us he'd always have our backs no matter what situations life put us in. It was something so simple and fun that consumed so much time with 5 kids in the house, but we never saw that we were actually learning to trust. For legal reasons and because I always want my family to remain the coolest family in history I cant really go into details about the kinds of trust falls we had. I will say imagine you are walking up a straight staircase and behind you your father says to stop, and not fall but sit! Actually sit down, that was my biggest dare and it took me forever to do, but perfectly placed behind me was a chair my father was holding up. He would not only always be there to catch me if I fell, but to support me and hold me up when I needed to rest a while.

The Teenage Years: A Spoiled Princess

By the time high school rolled around using the word spoiled to describe me was an understatement. I was a true Princess to the core. My Dad knew me and accepted every part of me even when it wasn't good. I remember him taking me to the Unifest in the city, there was food, drinks, music and a whole lot of fun to be had. I ran into some girls from school and wanted to go off by myself to enjoy the day with my friends. The plan was to spend the night at Pumpkin's house with the girls, and call him in the morning to come pick me up. However we had other things on the agenda that night like sneaking out while her mom was sleep. We went out partying and I had my drink ever. Hennessy and coke was smooth enough for a beginner trying to act like a big girl, but my second cup was straight Hennessy. Without knowing it I had met, reached, and exceeded my limit within a matter of minutes. I don't remember much else about that night. There was a park, it was dark, we were trying to get me stable enough to sneak back in. That was a mission impossible, we were spotted and busted straight through the door. Pumpkin's Mom called my Dad and told him what was going on and he came right away. Turned out he knew her parents and they ended up catching up on old times before he took me home. When we got in he didn't yell, he wasn't

mad, he gave me some Aleve and told me he'd
see me in the morning. That opened the door to
complete honesty between us because he
couldn't protect what he didn't know about, and i
believed he would always protect me no matter
what. We never had to relive that night because I
learned the ways I put myself in danger and
vowed to never do it again. I would always be
present when a drink was poured and know
exactly what went into it, I would sip and not try
to impress anyone who thought I couldn't drink,
and most importantly I would always have a ride
on stand bye who knew where i was and who i
was with. My sweet 16 was epic on every end.
My mom gave me a surprise party with all my
friends from church, and my dad took me and
my boyfriend on a dinner cruise. We had
Champagne and Shrimp Cocktail and danced
under the stars. I was always ahead of my years
but this took the cake. I had matured to a level of
fooling a whole cruise staff into thinking i was
over 21 and supposed to be partying that hard.
With me on a whole new level he took our
family game to the next level as well and started
Trust to the Next Level. This game was a
straight fear factor, trust, and haunted mansion
type experience all rolled into one and we
couldn't wait until the sun fell to play it. As my
teen years

were coming to a close I got one more go at
being the most spoiled daughter anyone could
imagine. He finally remarried A Strong,
Beautiful, Wise Woman and I just had to a part
of every step of this journey. After the wedding
talks of where we would we Honeymoon was
being discussed and once they settled on
Atlantic City also known as mini Vegas back in
the day I knew I had to go. So I packed my bags
and enjoyed the beginning of a wonderful union.
Yes you heard me right I went on My Father and
Step Mother's Honeymoon, and we had a ball.

California Dreaming

I know it looks bad but i promise he's not always
like that.
Girl you know how these men get, gotta be The
King 24/7 honey
He just had too much to drink tonight thats all
It's been really stressful these last couple of
months
Business is slow, and i try to help in any way I
can but sometimes it's just not enough.
He says I spend it twice as fast as I make it
We always need more shit tho and I'm who he
sends to take it
The fast life is fun and rewarding
Trips, Shopping Sprees, Partying Every Night.
How naive I used to be to think this was a life i
could live forever
I thought if I just never asked and did what I was
told I'd always be taken care of
I wore shades to mask the fear in my eyes as I
changed coasts
Fully knowing the extent of our relationship and
how it had drastically shifted
I was riding high on the dreams you sold me
Even higher with the best Cali bud in our brand
new house

This was paradise, heaven on earth, certified
billable bliss
Then I awoke broke, desperate, and alone
Surrounded by constant questions about
California
But what could i say....
It Was All A Dream

An Assassin's Asset

I was born a Bonnie
Always wanting more, Always searching for
better
Never stopping to think about the people i hurt
along the way
Just mind locked in to the man I loved
For him I would do anything, say anything, Be
anything
And he loved that
If I loved him enough he would never have to
get his hands dirty again
He would groom me, shape me, mold me until
my heart was as black as his
And then would come the tests
Send me out knowing nothing, while he threw
things in my path to make me fall
If I didn't it was Christmas everyday
Shopping sprees, Vacations, Cars, Houses,
Whatever I could dream up he would buy it for
me.
But just as sweet as he could be the dark side
was much worse
I wouldn't hear from him for days on end, and
when he would come around it was like he didn't
even know me.

He conditioned my mind to want to keep him
happy so when someone stood in the way of
that... they had to go
I had to make sure no one would ever hurt us
If I did my job and played my part my world
was set
As long as I could stay as dangerous as he was
he loved me
Problem is a Killer is only as good as his
weapon, and weapons don't think
But I did. I dared to think something other than
what he told me i was thinking
And it almost cost me my life

Change

It's time for a change
Things are evolving everyday
Don't know where you're going on your journey,
I don't know where you've been, but no matter
the battle, just know that every war comes to an
end.
Just keep moving forward, don't look back, drop
all your worries, he's got your back.
If you just focus on you, you won't lack.
If he did it for Me he can do it for you, I know it
looks hard, but I've seen the proof.
When you follow your truth there's nothing you
can't do.
I woke up today, my life is getting better I've
owned that.
I got to count my blessings, got to learn lessons,
life is only testing I know that.
With everything they throw at me and
everything they say about me it only makes me
smarter.
Can't you see that he's reshaping me?
I just put one foot in front of the other, I looked
up and I discovered the only one who could fix
it wasn't me.

So I had to make a change things are evolving
everyday.
If I can change my ways, then I know you can
do the same.
You can change for you, you can live your truth.
If I can change my ways, then I know you can
do the same.
You can change for you, you can be that proof.
It's time to make a change things are evolving
everyday.

A Different Kind of Love: Part One

Destiny:

It had been quite a year for me and I deserve to get away. All I wanted was to fill the sunshine on my gorgeous skin and not be blinded by a thousand flashing lights. Are we cruise to Fiji was exactly what I needed. As I unloaded the last of my luggage a sense of inspiration ran through my bones, I was going to take this break and truly unwind. My sister would insist that my entire life was one big vacation but that's just the image, being a club promoter and social figure was exhausting. Every minute of my night was carefully planned out, I wore clothes picked out for me, also hung out and took pictures with people also chosen to promote a certain look. From strip clubs to casinos every opening wanted the "flirtatious D Hollow" seen in their reviews. To the world D Hollow was the woman who men fell to their knees for but destiny Holloway couldn't keep a man to save her life. I had never had a relationship that lasted longer than 6 months and my entire 25 years of life. I had never told any man I love him and most of all I had never been swept off of my feet. I slid into a sexy red bikini and hit the deck. No sooner than I sat in my lounge chair and pulled my shades to the top of my head the cupid not only shoot me but practically smack the taste out of my mouth. Before I knew it I was staring mouth gaping wide open at the absolute sexiest man I have ever seen. When our eyes met I felt a jolt of electricity shoot up my thighs causing me to cross my legs. I reapplied my shades and licked my lips. He was mine, I was in love, and I didn't even know his name...

Stephon:

To think I could have been going home to a nagging crazy pregnant girlfriend but instead I was toasting to a fully all expense paid week-long cruise. All I had to do was 8 2 hours sessions to a day for 4 days and any private sessions I booked outside of that was extra money in my pocket! I called my homie to thank him for backing out of this at the last minute. I wanted to celebrate my freedom with a victory lap so I headed up to the main deck. As I walked out in my red Speedo I could feel the eyes of every lady I passed and I loved it. Just as I finish the lap I caught the most gorgeous set of hazel green eyes locked in on me. I flashed her winning smile and grabbed my towel. Before heading to the shower I grabbed an activity list from the bar circled my session later that day, then slid it beside her as I walked past. I knew I had to see those thick thighs covered in sweat. Just as expected she was the first one through the door. An extended hand and a million dollars smile is what I got along with her name... Destiny Holloway. She looked so familiar like I had seen her in every dream I ever had. As soon as she put her hand and mine I knew I would never go back. Keisha would be fine but my destiny was destiny. I booked a midnight session with her and vowed that I would give all hey muscles a good workout! She proved to be very flexible and we both prove to be very much attracted to each other. The last night of the cruise we lay under the stars and she whispered "Stephon I think I love you". I was hooked...

Destiny:
I couldn't believe I had given that man the cookie on the first date. Technically it wasn't a date but it sure felt like one. Stephon Washington had me wide open. The things he did to my body you would think we'd known each other all of our lives. He told me he was in a transition and looking for a new start so exactly two weeks after that first amazing workout he was moving into my condo. This relationship had taken me by surprise and for

once I was being swept off of my feet. He was everything I never had. He was so sweet and supportive. He didn't judge me for my job and he even helped a lot. My new bow was all anyone could talk about and he was getting so much business that we decided to open a gym together. Making money with my honey was the best but that quickly changed. For once I understood how men felt when they had to deal with other men all over me because of my job. I'm not a jealous woman by far, I had it going on and I knew it but the chicks were determined to try me when it came to my man. We were all about our paper and business but I could tell he was starting to feel himself. Social media is a hell of a drug and he was a junkie. It was my job to always be seen and have a bunch of people throwing me on their social media pages but I was used to it and it was just a job. I didn't spend every minute with my phone attached to my hand reading and commenting on everything I saw and it was getting beyond annoying. One day I was in the office managing our accounts and I heard a loud commotion out on the floor so I go check it out. As I stepped into the room a woman holding a newborn baby. With an infant and a stroller, and three other kids standing by looked me in my face and said "Oh I see, so this is the reason you missed the birth of your child!

Well since you're out here playing house now
you can have this one too" shoving the newborn
in Stephon's arms then pointing her ratchet red
stiletto nails in my face she said "and you can
make that monthly check out to Keisha Davis"

A Different Kind of Love: Part Two

Stephon:

Life was really starting to look great for me I had an amazing sexy woman who believed in all my dreams and pushed me into fulfilling my goals. We opened my gym together and I loved her beyond words for that. After I got on my feet Destiny started to change. She constantly complained about my fans and all the time I was spending on social media with them, but I was just trying to be the man she needed. I know she hated the spotlight and clubbing every weekend. With the money I made at the gym plus the appearances she would never have to put on another fake smile for anyone. I loved Destiny Holloway but I didn't think she knew just how much. I had completely left Keisha and the kids behind and giving destiny all the things Keisha wanted out of me. Just as I was beginning to enjoy our new life and walks my past. Keisha stormed in my session like a hurricane screaming and yelling with all the kids in tow. And then Destiny shows up, I didn't even know she was here. Keisha shoved my newborn into my arms and strolled out just as loud as she rolled in. I could see the tears welling up in the corners of Destiny's eyes, but she held them in and kept her cool. She took the baby from my arms and said we talked when I got home. The day never passed so slowly and after I assured out the last of our members and locked up I've raced straight home. When I walked in the house it was full of boxes and bags for the baby and my woman was sitting on the floor. A glass of red wine and one hand and a fat spliff in the other with the face full of tears brought me to my knees. "Baby I'm so sorry I didn't tell you... please don't leave me"

Destiny:
After Keisha left I took the baby from Stephon and told him to carry on with business. I walked back into my office and sunk into my plush desk chair. How could he keep this secret from me was all of those kids his, what kind of mother just drops her newborn off with a man that ups and leaves her, would he ever do that to me? My mind was racing with so many questions I thought my head would explode. I snatched the receiver off the hook and dialed our assistant Natasha. "Hey Nat can you go out and bring me a car seat / stroller set for a newborn quickly please, I have to get out of here" was what I said when she picked up. Sure enough 10 minutes

later she was strolling into my office and told me the car seat was set up and ready for me to use. I placed baby Washington in the stroller and headed out to my car. As I passed the weight room I could see Stephon with a pain look on his face. Thank God he didn't see me cuz I wasn't ready to face this problem head on. Instead I loaded the baby whose name I didn't even know in my car and hit every mall I could think of. By the time we finished shopping me and little man had become the best of friends. He wrapped his little fingers around my pinky as I sat in a rocking chair and fed him a bottle. After I put him to sleep I laid him in the middle of our bed and surrounded him with pillows. I went into the kitchen and grabbed my biggest wine glass and filled it to the brim, then pulled out one of our pre-rolls and slid to the floor. My tears must have given way to gravity as well because before I knew it I could barely see through the large drops of water consuming my eyes. I heard the door open and my heart dropped. Here it was, the time had come to get the answers I so desperately needed to get me through this. He fell to his knees at the side of me and we talked all night.

Stephon:

After a long night of talking and put in together baby furniture I was beyond exhausted mentally and physically. I went up to our bedroom and fed little Stevie and placed him in his new crib, then scoop Destiny up off the couch and carried her to our bed. The second she hit the sheets she nuzzled closer to me and drifted deeper into her sleep. I looked to the sky and silently thanked God for sending this Angel into my life. She was so patient and understanding, so calm and serene. She was nothing like any woman I had ever met before and I was determined to give her the world on a silver platter. She deserved nothing less than the best and now that all the secrets were out of the way I could finally give her all of me. The next day I called my homeboy so he could cover all of my sessions for the day while I spent some quality time with my family. We had turned our home office into Stevie's nursery overnight but Destiny wasn't pleased at all. She had always dreamed about her perfect family and the home filled with memories but this wasn't it. "He'll need a yard to grow up and playing and his own space not an office babe." So before lunch we were heading out to check out a few single family homes. This was nothing like buying a space for our gym. She was so picky and nothing we saw was good enough for what she called our forever home. Six houses later I could care less if the closets were the size of a matchbook or if the stove was gas or electric. As we pulled up to the seventh home I silently declared that this was the last house I would see today. From my lips to God's ears, Destiny's eyes lit up the moment she stepped out of the car. I knew I had found her forever home. Step one was complete and I became the man worthy to be Destiny Holloway's first and only love.

A Different Kind of Love: Part Three

Destiny:
Stephon took the next day off to spend time with me and the baby. Since we both had the whole day free I took that as the perfect time to go shopping for a proper home to raise a child in. For a newborn just the room with furniture and toys was fine but what about when Stevie started crawling around, what about his first steps, and would we really measure his growth on the door of our old office. Absolutely not, being the spoiled princess I was he had an agent and a whole list of at least 20 to 30 listings ready for me to review by noon. I crossed off about 9:00 and listed the others in order of proximity to the gym. On paper they all seemed wonderful but once I stepped inside most of those places didn't even compare to my condo. I wasn't just going to jump into anything. The backyards were subpar, the closets were a joke, the master baths look more like hotel bathrooms, and the kitchens were all missing that spark that made a woman want to cook all day. I could tell he was getting tired so I told him we could go eat after the next house. As I made my sixth huge X on the paper

a long yawn escaped my lips. He only drove for about 5 minutes before he drove through a huge gated community and onto a circle driveway. I was home, I knew it as soon as my Jimmy Choo's hit the pavement. The seven bedroom three story estate was made for me. The backyard set on a little over an acre alone and was fully equipped with a pool, hot tub, fire pit, brick set grill, and plenty of grass to build a playground and treehouse. Each bedroom was huge with its own walk-in closet and attached bathroom. The basement featured a movie theater, bowling alley, mini golf set, and a wet bar. And don't even get me started on the kitchen I could employ a staff of three for the kitchen alone. "This is it!" I told Stephon as I open the double doors to my master bath from heaven. He kissed the top of my head and told the broker "we'll take it offer the seller 10,000 over asking if we can have it as is". In the car he asked if I loved my forever home and I said "oh yeah babe! This place is amazing but your heart is my home."

Stephon:
After putting in a more than generous offer on the house I took my baby to her favorite restaurant Benihana's. She couldn't stop talking about how much she loved the place and

couldn't wait to move in, I was pretty excited myself. As we drove back to the condo our agent called to let us know the offer was accepted and we could pick up our keys first thing in the morning. I parked the car and went to the back to get Stevie but was beat to the punch by Destiny. She was so in love with the baby you would have thought she carried him for 9 months herself. I sat on the couch playing my video games and watching Destiny and the baby on the floor playing. A loud knock on the door startled us all and caused Stevie to start crying. She cradled him tightly in her arms as I went to open the door. No sooner than I turned the knob I was being handcuffed and forced into a cop car. "Why are you taking him! What's the charge?" I could hear her yelling from behind me. Keisha's crazy butt had pressed charges for kidnapping and child support. I couldn't believe I was ending such an amazing day in handcuffs. I guess the saying is true when you're at the top brace for the fall. Destiny was there bright and early looking good as ever and she told me she just hired the best lawyer and she would have me out in no time. The next day I arrived at my bail hearing to see my horrible ratchet baby mama disguised as a Susie homemaker. My jaw hit the floor as my lawyer walked in dressed in a badass black suit and red tie and my strong amazing sexy woman right behind her dressed in all white pants suit carrying my son in a red blinged out car seat on her arm like a purse. She was a boss in every sense of the word and nothing to be played with. She rubbed my back then cut her eyes over to Keisha and took her seat right behind me.

Destiny:

After watching my man being carried away in handcuffs I couldn't sleep a wink. I called my best friend Cameron Hollowell one of the city's best attorneys and told her what happened. She said he would have a bail hearing within 24 to 48 hours and we would be armed and ready when he did. I told her we needed full custody of not only Stevie but his 2-year-old daughter Daedra as well. Keisha showed up to court and the most ugly grandma dress I had ever seen trying to play the victim but my girl wasn't having that. She went straight in with the facts of the case, Keisha was unfit and literally forced her newborn on us and we had the video to prove it. Then she hit her with the sucker Punch we wanted physical custody of both children born from Stephon Washington. The judge put in an emergency family hearing for the next day, released my man, and gave Miss ratchet an earful about her behavior. He turned to me and kissed me deeply as soon as the gavel was banged. I took a few hundred dollar bills out of my bag and threw them to the ground as we walked past Keisha and said "here's something to hold you over... maybe even get you a better victim dress". Stephon just laughed and carried Stevie to the car. We drove straight to Cammie's office to prepare for tomorrow and he told me "babe I can't believe you and your bestie bust up in that courtroom like that this morning she was so shook". I laughed so hard this was the first time he was seeing my best friend out of her baggy sweats in the gym. We came up with a reasonable schedule for the kids and a more than reasonable monthly stipend offer. The next day family Court was a breeze turns out all she really wanted was the money so getting her to agree to our terms with all too easy. We got custody of Daedra and Stevie and she got two weekends out of a month and 500 per kid a month. He's not obligated to pay for her other three children but with $1,000 a month and us taking care of the youngest two she was fine.

A Different Kind of Love:
Part Four

Stephon:

My queen was everything any man could ever dream of. She truly loved me and supported me through anything. The thought of getting the kids had never crossed my mind, but she said why wouldn't we? You are their father and in a much better position to provide for them than she is right now. I knew at that very moment she was my wife. After I cut Keisha 15,000 check for back pay of 6 months on Stevie and 24 months on Daedra I kissed destiny on her cheek and walk to my car. I had a few stops to make before heading to our housewarming party the first stop was Tiffany's to drop a small fortune on the Tiffany's solstice cushion engagement ring. It was very specific on my baby's vision board this was her dream not one like it, this one! I could almost hear her cute little voice in my head as I swipe my black card the next stop was Qdoba for her Hispanic bar. She ordered nachos, hard & soft tacos, tortilla bowls, chicken, shrimp, steak, all the fixings, and tons of queso. The only reason I was even here was because we had finally settled on doing two culturally themed mini bars instead of the many Thanksgiving she originally wanted. Her Italian pasta bar would be no problem with her state-of-the-art kitchen that had to have a pasta maker, but the Hispanic bar quickly changed when she got to all the toppings she had to make and it not being complete without her favorite queso. So Qdoba was stuck making an overnight Hispanic bar. The last stop before I pulled into the driveway was the bakery to get the cake. I parked and quickly hid the blue bag and my glove compartment, then started to carry my love her food. The party was in full swing and everyone was enjoying themselves this was the first party that she ever got to call her own shots so trying to hijack the spotlight with mission impossible. But then she cleaned her glass to get everyone's attention. As soon as she thanked our guests I dropped to my knee and began to ask the most beautiful, intelligent, charismatic, witty woman in the whole wide world to marry me. "...In short I'll give you the world Destiny Holloway if you become Mrs Destiny Washington. Will you marry me?"

Destiny:
After we left family Court I had to rush the kids back home and get the place ready for our housewarming party. I had all of the things that

didn't fit in my vision of the house shipped off to storage and replaced with soft Elegance hatches. I definitely had to have our new space already for when my man came home. I put the finishing touches on the decorations and set up the table for my Italian / Mexican feast. While Stevie slept and Daedra played in their room I made fettuccine, penne, and stuffed ravioli noodles with ground beef, chicken, and shrimp, with basil tomato, cheesy alfredo, and avocado pesto sauces. Then I carried the kids upstairs to get ready. I went into the huge his and hers closet and picked out a cute pink leopard print tutu, a black and pink big sister shirt, and some black jeans for Daedra, and a black baby brother onesie for Stevie. After my shower and their bath we all got dressed. All of our family and friends showed up to shower us with love and gifts for our new home. My parents fell in love with the kids right away and said they would gladly take the babies on the weekends so we could have alone time. This party was the beginning of a new life for me for once I was planning and overseeing the party and it was for me and my accomplishments. No one's telling me what to wear or drink or do just me doing me and loving it. I clinked my glass to raise a toast and Stephon got down on one knee with the sweetest proposal ever then pulled out my dream rock! I almost fainted it looks so much bigger in real life I screamed yes about a million times and jumped up and down. This was truly the best day of my life. I couldn't wait to start planning my special day, it would be a fairy tale wedding fit for A queen. Stephon's mom hugged me so tight and told me I was the daughter she had always wanted. I promised her and my mom that we would go dress shopping soon. For the rest of the night all everybody could talk about was how wonderful we look together and how amazing my ring was.

Stephon:
After the party Destiny dived head first into planning our wedding. Every time I saw her face pop up on my screen I knew it was about the wedding. She was an amazing mother so I never got calls about the kids she treated them as if they were her own. Her days were now filled with Doctor appointments, Mommy and me classes, and a whole lot of shopping. I thought she was bad with just Stevie but adding Daedra to the mix was beyond crazy. That woman bought them everything every child in America wanted. Daedra was our spoiled little princess, every day I came home she ran into my arm screaming "Daddy" and after about a million kisses she'd say "give Mama a kiss too she..."

Everyday it's a different reason, but the one thing that never changes is the love and adoration in her voice for her mama. It was so clear the bond that Destiny had with my children just came naturally for her. She didn't try to buy their love she also showered them with attention and affection. We never had to talk about when she wanted to start a family of her own because this was her family. Having a woman like Destiny Holloway made me sure there was a God and he was amazing. Even when I was undeserving he still chose to shine down on me with exactly what I've dreamed of. My grandmother always told me baby the day your wife walks into your life will be forever burned into your brain and heart. You will be able to tell your children that story for years and years and never get tired of reliving it. If you ever find yourself annoyed at the thought of any part of that day she's not the one. looking back that was one of the best days of my life and I'm sure I will remember every detail of it for years to come. Destiny and our mothers had a shopping date so dangerous Stevie and Daddy had the whole day to ourselves. Today was my grandmother's birthday so I strap the kids in and went to get my first love some flowers and balloons, I really wish she was still here with us. She would have been so proud of my choice to marry Destiny, I imagine they would be the best of friends because I saw so much of her inside of Destiny. This woman was just a breath of fresh air, life should never be this easy and carefree. I was so used to working so much harder than everyone else just to get by, now I was a business and homeowner and about to marry the woman of my dreams. To save my life changed drastically since meeting Destiny would be a huge understatement, she made my world complete. The future Mrs Washington was so worthy of the name. Strong, beautiful, and intelligent just like the women who raised me. Even at her worst I loved her beyond all comprehension. She was turning into a true bridezilla right before my eyes but it was so cute. Everything had to be perfect on her wedding day and I understood her. She told me I am only getting married once this one day has to capture a lifetime of dreams and transcend into a beautiful lifetime of memories. I want to get teary eyed every time I open our wedding album and look back at our special day. She was the most sane bridezilla I had ever witnessed. Even when she got the most over the top ideas she always had a way of making it sound so necessary. It also helped that every place she called was thrilled to be a part of her special day and offered her mad discounts. I stopped at my grandmother's favorite bakery and picked up two red velvet cupcakes then took the kids for a picnic date with their memaw. We sat and listened to her favorite music while we ate some good old soul food. I looked at my children then to the sky and said "Grandma I miss you so much everyday. I hope you're proud of the man I've become, you always pushed me and believed in my dreams and I finally found a woman who makes my soul smile. I know you'd love Destiny, all I ask is that you shine down on us on her special day." Just as a silence tear rolled down my face I felt a hand on my shoulder she said "I know she's proud of you baby and shining in your life daily." I was stunned to my beautiful fiance tracked me down when my mother told her what today was. We smiled and laughed as I shared all the great memories I had with my grandmother. Then we sang Happy Birthday, ate the cupcakes, and went home to put our children in the bed. Destiny Holloway soon to be Washington had finally met the original and it was now complete for me.

A Different Kind of Love:
Part Five

Destiny:

I was about to marry the man of my dreams and everything had to be just right. With all the connections I thought it would be a cakewalk but I quickly regretted not hiring a real wedding planner. I had my checklist and my man, he was so helpful but I knew this wasn't his cup of tea. He could care less if we had a band or DJ so we ended up with both. The one thing he requested was that red velvet be our cake flavor. With everything else left to me to choose this wedding was becoming more over the top each day. The date was closing in fast and worrying so much about all the details I missed one of the most important parts, the wedding party. I had no idea who he plans to have by his side and outside of my best friend and maid of honor I didn't know who'd be by mine either. I had stuff on up to solve this huge dilemma. When he answered his cell I could hear Keisha screaming in the background. I'm on my way it's all I could get out before I rushed the kids to Mrs. Clemson's house and sped all the way to my gym. When I opened the door she was yelling in my receptionist's face and trying to get past her. I quickly grabbed her arm with so much force it would have popped out of the socket if she tried to resist. Once we were standing on the street she looked me up and down. Since she was clearly stuck I spoke up "what the hell are you doing here? This is a place of business not a damn broth." She pulled out the cutest Tiffany blue bracelet box and held it up with her eyebrows raised. Stephon stepped out and said "that's an invitation most people say thank you or sorry I can't make it!" She yelled "why the fuck would you send me an invitation to watch you marry the bitch that ruined our family." Just then all I saw was read as I slap the taste out of her mouth. "Ruined! Sweetie he was done with you before I ever stepped into the picture. And because of me you can keep your lights on and your children failed while I do your job with his. And I invited you, I figured you would want to show a united front for your children but I see your content playing the ghetto baby mama roll." She threw the box at my feet and said "fuck whatever you think you know about me just cuz you buy a crib don't make you a mother! Holla at me when you have your own if you even can". Stephon must have caught me mid-air cuz I swear I launched every part of my body at her. Now I understand why he hated her so much, she just had a way of leaving a bad taste in your mouth. Holding me in his arms he gave her the sternest look I had ever seen in my life, she turned and walked away and I melted in his firm powerful embrace. He kissed the top of my forehead and said "I got you Dee, always". Once I got myself together I drove straight home to the kids. Honestly having them around brought power, purpose, love, and inspiration to my life everyday. I love teaching and guiding them, and of course dressing them in the cutest clothes. But it was deeper than that, I loved for the first time and was somehow blessed with two beautiful children. Of course I would give my husband as many children as he wanted but for now I was fine with my family of four and so was he. As the days drag by we decided we wanted a small intimate party of five plus us made seven, my Maid of Honor and best friend Cammie, and Matron of Honor my sister Tay would be escorted by his Best Man and brother Sam then my bestie Jojo with his best friend who was also the reason we met, Anthony. The wedding itself was already big enough with a guest list of 1,500 confirmed and growing. I had a cathedral service planned so the trip to the front would be insane and because his grandmother would have wanted a church wedding. And trust me it was one of the most expensive places to dress up in

all fresh white and pink roses but it was so worth
it. The reception hall was the hardest thing ever
to find it had to be big enough not only to seat
over 2,000 people but have a huge stage and
enough room for my magical waterfall ring for
my first dance. Not to mention room for a band,
DJ, a huge buffet, and a full bar. Nothing was
going to stop my shine my day would be
elegant, dramatic, entertaining, and full of so
much love.

Stephon:
The day had finally come and I was getting more
nervous as the minutes passed. I had heard all
the horror stories about cold feet and run away
brides but I knew that could never happen to me
and Destiny. We were made to be together and
nothing would stop that. But for some reason I
couldn't shake this feeling of terror. My boy
walked in and said "Yo! The wedding party just
walked past! Crazy, now I know why it's only
three of them who else could possibly stand in
that line". Me and Sam bust out laughing.
Anthony was a fool, he kept us laughing all the
time. If the ladies were heading down the halls it
was getting close to Showtime. I sent my boys to
the opposite side and went to take my place at
the altar. I held it together as My Angel made
her way to me and we sealed the deal with a

kiss. For the rest of the night Mrs. Washington was on cloud nine with a permanent smile on her face. I thought her face would eventually tired but then I remembered who I married, that woman could smile for days. We stepped onto this risen black ring in the middle of the dance floor and the show began. There was a shower flow of water with lights and messages in the water plus the ring was slowly spinning. The massive red velvet cake surely stole the show too. It was beautiful, elegant, and massive, but the most moist cake I ever been into. We danced The night away in each other's arms and I couldn't wait to whisk my wife away from everyone and make more magical memories as husband and wife this time on our week long cruise to Fiji. As we said our goodbyes and family and friends flooded the entryway with bubbles and confetti I got that weird feeling again. I clutched these hands tighter and ushered her into our limo. As soon as the car pulled off I attacked my wife like a wild animal, I was all over I didn't even hear the privacy window coming down but I heard Destiny's scream ringing in my ears as pain ripped through my back. My wife cradled my face in her lap and I closed my eyes as the darkness overtook my body...

Destiny:

As I was gliding through the night on my husband's arm it was truly a breathtaking scene with a majestic regal feeling in the air. You would have thought we were Jay Z and Beyoncé when we exited the building. The lights were flashing and confetti was being thrown all over us. We got into the limo Stephon couldn't get enough of me. He was sending sweet passionate kisses down my neck then I saw the privacy glass sliding down. Before I could compose myself three shots rang out so loud and I could feel my husband's full weight crushed against me. I screamed so loud and within a matter of seconds Anthony was trying to soothe me from the driver's seat and keep his best friend holding on to life as he rushed us to the hospital in the now empty limousine. I cradled his face and told him it would be okay. Anthony sped right to the emergency door at the hospital and Stephon was rushed off before I even got a chance to tell him I left him. After filling out in this papers I paced back and forth for hours waiting to hear that my husband was still alive and would be fine. When the doctor finally came out I shot up out of my chair and rushed over to him "is he okay? Please tell me he made it through surgery! Can I see him?" I said frantically. He just grabbed my hands and begin his bad news feel... "Mrs

Washington your husband was shot three times at close range we were able to remove all the bullets but there was a lot of swelling. He's in a coma but we believe he will pull through this. I am so sorry ". Thank God his mother was at my side because as soon as he said coma my legs gave way and buckled. She bent down gently letting me sink and kissed my forehead. Sam came over to us and scooped me up in his arms like his brother should have carried me over the threshold and I just lost it. He just held firm and let me get it all out while he shed silent tears for his baby brothers condition. He walked over to our mom and said " ma I'm going to take her to the house the girls are waiting on her. You got everything you need for the kids right? " When she nodded he turned around and headed towards the door weekly I managed to say " let's say good night before we leave." I kissed my sleeping husband and wished upon a star that he found his way home to me.

www.ingramcontent.com/pod-product-compliance
Lightning Source LLC
LaVergne TN
LVHW011037200726

843509LV00011B/1303